Scarlet & Shadows

Scarlet & Shadows

A collection of poetry on trauma
and healing

by

Sarah Blakely

For anyone who struggles with anger at a world not built for them.

Your struggle is valid.

Preface

This book explores topics of sexual assault, trauma, survival, and feminine rage.
It serves as a sort of sequel to my debut collection, *Volcano Girl*.
I hope this collection not only enrages you, but also takes you on a journey where you can explore that anger in a healthy way, and question the systems of our world that enable abuse.

If you've been bottling up your anger and quieting yourself, this book is for you.

Trigger Warning

This book contains content relating to certain topics that may be triggering to readers.
Please exercise self-care before and after reading.

Sexual assault/abuse

Mental illness and suicidal ideations

Self-harm

Contents

Trauma Draws Blood

2

Pluto In Capricorn, As A Capricorn Rising

For sixteen years, I was pursued
by a devil-horned god, in a series of crude
power-hungry and lusty attacks,
assault after assault on my body,
vile, violation after violation,
the spirit of Pan in every man I crossed,
inducing panic attacks as years pass,
goring me repeatedly for sport.

It's no coincidence that I was hunted
throughout his woods by his pack of rabid
      canines,
all deer in the headlights eyes and delicious,
thick, juicy thighs on bone,
mad beasts all begging for a taste of my
      sweet flesh.
I still have scars, though the bites have
      healed,
I still have wounds that my hands can't feel
festering inside.

Sarah Blakely

He took my victimized voice and played it
        like a pipe,
a dog whistle screaming,
my sad cries turned into fluttering
        harmonies,
the trophy of a conquered woman.
He danced and frolicked as I wailed and
        howled,
sounds persuaded into sadistic satyr songs.
He didn't expect the wind, however,
to pick up and play the untainted truth.

Riot Of My Body

He stormed my body like a riot
pounding at my doors,
breaking his way through,
shattering glass,
ravaging my heart.

Sarah Blakely

The Places I Survived Being A Woman

Sydney Street,
near my old elementary school,
the curb next to the abandoned house
that my soul became.

Alamitos Avenue,
a molding beach motel
with stains from gas station slushies,
lies of citrus taste.

A cold metal park bench
along the railroad tracks,
drunken stumbling down stairs and giggling,
crawdads gossiping.

Johnson Avenue,
where the creek cuts across,
lies a lonely looming lair
of lust and latex.

An offshoot of Doris Avenue,
somewhere in the baywood area,
dank bud and bassy dubstep beats dropping,
tie dye tapestries.

Mustang Village,
under a bunk bed,
off white walls, ping pong balls bouncing,
cards on the table.

The house on the hill
overlooking the ocean,
on a night as black as my memory,
4 a.m. calls for help.

The lawn of the Methodist church
by the bay where the boats linger
in the mud like they've never seen the ocean,
fog rolls in.

Hayward House,
just barely off campus,
across from the glamorous university track,
dim hallway staircase.

Sarah Blakely

Stadium Park,
opposite my friend's apartment,
she made waffles that tasted of disbelief,
building a wall between us.

Bennett Avenue,
overlooking Belmont shore,
lights at night glimmering specs in a black
      ocean,
drowning wine and couch cushions.

Laurel Hill park,
where the grass starts to slope,
hiding in darkness the streetlights don't
      reach,
claws crawling up my skirt.

A garage in Cottage Gove,
on top of a yacht we'd just towed,
stumbling around like a mermaid on new
      drunken legs,
spread across the bow.

15th Avenue,
apartment number 3,
loudly and violently dragged to my bloody
        bed,
tucking me in with teeth.

Somewhere along Amazon and 26th,
face buried in a mattress,
with my hope for mankind in the graveyard
        with it,
another dinner date to domesticate.

Shoreline shopping center,
along the waterfront where the boats sway,
adventures with exotic men with tongues of
        tequila,
shattered mosaic artwork.

Sarah Blakely

My Hometown Is A Museum
after Jasmine S. Higgins

My hometown is a museum
of rape culture history on display.
Sydney street, my first assault,
the sushi restaurant on Marsh street,
where the grooming began.
The hallways of the middle school,
lakeside views on foggy mornings,
where my best friend became a beast.
The bench by the railroad tracks
where he crawled on top of me,
the one in the park is haunted too.
The secret place we used to call "Nam"
where we shared that bottle of moonshine
became a grove of nightmares for me.
The bike path I walked home one day
when I was being followed downtown,
even my childhood home is cursed by him.
A tranquil winter view of the full moon
over the hill from my window
takes me back to traumatized times.

April Showers

They say April showers bring May flowers
but in my case it carried a taste so sour,
hands at my neck, he ordered me to swallow,
turned me into a corpse, an empty shell so
       hollow.

Staring at the moon outside this fogged up
       hell,
pressing my palm to the window, ignoring
       the smell,
pounding at the glass, but nobody is out
       there,
nobody to save me from his twisted glare.

My hand sinks, creating a small handprint,
condensation tears run down my wrist, a hint
at my future, crying in therapy for years to
       come
all because of one sick piece of living scum.

Sarah Blakely

With The Moon As My Witness

What will the moon say
when she sees you acting this way?
Her pure white light contrasts
against my loss of innocence.
My grasping hands
reach for her subtle beams
but fall short
by a few hundred thousand miles.
She sees your vicious fists,
hitting, groping, demeaning,
she watches it all
through the windows of your truck.
With the moon as my witness,
I am tainted.

The Ghost Of Marie LeRoy

Abused at such a young
tender age,
leaving her parents filled
with endless rage,
demanding he hang,
wanting his head on a post,
declaring him guilty
of turning their daughter into a ghost.

I know this trauma,
I know this pain,
vengeful and hateful,
calling for criminal chains.
This wound flows, aching,
through my maternal blood,
a genetic modification,
mutating my lifepath with mud.

This woman is my ancestor,
a branch of my family tree,
I'm pulling up the roots
and finding some to be diseased.
I've washed my body ten thousand times,
thinking I could remove his mark,
but it turns out the healing I really need
is within my own bark.

Piercing

I met an apparition of a man,
a foggy figure at the pier,
among misty memories
of a moldy old motel room
featuring frightening florals
within wicked walls
I won't be able to return to.

My memory is cotton cloth
full of holes chewed out by trauma moths,
I feel them biting into me
cutting out patterns,
paper snowflakes made with hate.

All I remember is his pierced tongue
a silver stud, metallic taste,
or maybe it was blood on my lips
as he pierced into me.

Medusa

God of the sea,
he knew better than me,
young and naive,
defiled, I grieved.

My hair grew to snakes,
one for every mistake
of entrusting a man
with my heart in his hands.

My eyes drained to grey,
turning men into clay,
if any wandering eye
settled to spy.

Goddess gave me wings,
though my looks might sting,
there is power in my glare,
making men run scared.

For now I learned
that protection is earned.

Bouquet Of Wilted Flowers

He plucked me so coarsely,
for his bouquet of wilted flowers,
damaged and delicate,
he knew he had power.
As he clutched our stems tightly,
we trembled and cowered.

Sarah Blakely

You Left Me Bloody Like The Brick Buildings At The Downtown Centre

This cold corridor is troubled and tainted,
red brick buildings bloodied and painted.
New shops and restaurants line the walls,
forgetting your presence, but I recall
walking in a group with you leading the way,
your herd of girls blindly following anything
      you say.
You befriended us all, a wolf in sheep's
      clothing,
it's disturbing to think you were really just
      probing,
hunting for your prey, a few tasty bites,
you knew you had our trust so we wouldn't
      fight.
We weren't prepared to see you off to jail,
later receiving your prison letters in the mail.
Love notes and promises you never intended
      to keep,
you fed us lies to keep us quietly asleep.

Silently believing, slowly bleeding,
you must've heard me begging and pleading,
asserting a boundary you'd blurred and
        diluted,
yet you took me whenever it suited.

Cemetery Weather

I never knew what I would do
if anybody tried to speak your name.

I would cringe,
my body would tremble and flinch,
a spastic allergic reaction.
I would choke,
my throat would close up,
remembering the strength of your hands
       around it.
I would cry,
my eyes would drown,
allowing an escape from seeing your face.

I never knew what I would do
if anybody tried to take you away.

I would defend you,
my mind would forget the harm you caused,
because we were best friends,
weren't we?

If Someone Told You Your Best Friend Was A Monster, Would You Listen?

They all warned me
about the monster in the shadows,
saying I should keep my distance,
telling me not to drink in
his honey whiskey words
that burned with his bite at my neck.

They warned me
about the demon in the dark,
all greed and force,
leading me down a gaslit path,
illuminating his alternate reality
that blackened my world like charcoal.

They warned me
about the vampire and his teeth,
crimson-stained against pearly white,
taking samples from his victims,
taste-testing and traumatizing,
and locking them up in his lair.

But nobody warned me
about the familiar I called "friend,"
the beast beside me, a leech, a lover.
He drained my spirit like blood
till my veins ran dead and dry,
and then he moved on to the next.

From The Eyes Of A Discarded Doll

"Look, don't touch,"
"Keep your hands to yourself,"
rules that only seem to apply
to valuables on the shelf,
but when my body
was left on the table,
your grabby hands took it
because they were able.

You left your grimy fingerprints
all over my pretty porcelain skin,
you couldn't see my value though,
just used me up and tossed me in the bin.
You declared me trash
and threw me away,
dropped me into a world
of death and decay,
where rats and other scum
like you
take bites from my figure,
little pieces to chew.

Sarah Blakely

All that's left of this
ceramic shell
are chips and splinters,
remnants of my personal hell.

They Saw It With Their Own Eyes But Did Nothing

I remember nothing about that night
but your sloppy grip on my hips,
bobbing up and down as you thrusted
into my unconscious body.
I wonder if I was moaning.
Or if you even realized
that you were fucking a corpse,
revealing your necrophiliac desires
to everyone else in the room.
Their judging eyes chastising,
blaming my body, or the alcohol,
or both.
But never you.
They all looked the other way
and pretended not to notice
the rape happening in the room.

Sarah Blakely

The Rape Of A Monarch

He had her pinned
on the ground.
My first thoughts
upon seeing him
on top of her,
her still, motionless body,
was if she was okay.

If she wanted it.
If she said yes.
If she was enjoying it.
If she knew there was a crowd
watching them.
If she felt ashamed.

A man jokes,
"Give them some privacy!"
Everyone laughs,
spectators at this sport
called rape culture.

I've been there too,
dear butterfly,
the pain will fly with me
forever.

Sarah Blakely

Snow Is No Longer Innocent

I vaguely remember December
after you cursed me forever.
It snowed a week later,
a rare symbolic souvenir
of innocence and youth stolen away.
Alone at 18.

I walked to the park after dark
in a foot of cold fluff at my frigid feet.
The steps to the entrance of the sanctuary
reminded me of how I imagined Narnia
in a childhood untainted by bloody lust,
a pure white path illuminated at night.

I marveled at the wintry wonderland
even with no moon to brighten the sky,
the snow glowed softly in the dark,
guiding me forward, step by slushy step,
to the comforts of solitude, serenity,
I walk through the gates to adulthood.

I Was A Hole Of A Woman

I was a cave,
he was the bear hibernating inside.
I was a mine,
he was the miner digging for gold.
I was a grave,
for his corpse to rest in.
I was a hole in the earth
he felt the need to fill.

Scars Left Behind

Okay

Sometimes I feel like
I'm okay
and then I remember
what happened
and I realize
I simply forgot
that I wasn't okay.

Sarah Blakely

Fully Alive

If I were truly
fully alive,
it wouldn't feel like torture
just to survive.
Operating just barely,
in motion but slowly.

Grateful

I am not grateful for my trauma.
It didn't make me stronger.
Anxiety invalidated me,
until I shattered.
Shame pinned me down,
crushed my spirit.
Depression held me back for years,
stagnant, stuck, stale.

Their actions don't deserve a thank you.

Peter Pan

Trauma is the villainous hooked hand
reaching out to snag me, to hold me back.
Keeping me in this fairy cage,
tormented by endless flashbacks.
Triggered too often by little intimacies,
provoking my brain to panic.
Stuck in this skeleton with a buried key,
locked up tight for eternity.
I feel I'll never grow old,
at least not mentally.
I'm trapped in my past
like Peter Pan in Neverland.
A lost child stuck in this
adult body.

Grenades

What if I was shaking
not because I was cold,
but because the thing
you asked me to hold,
exploded between my fingers,
leaving me, shrapnel, exposed,
triggered by traumatic memories of those
grenades I've swallowed
for the sake of a man.

Scarlet & Shadows

For some reason
my memories
of that night are
painted in shades
of scarlet and
shadows.

The Man With The Silver-Studded Tongue

He tiptoes around in my brain,
though I can't remember his name.
His face is blurry, though the studded silver
through his tongue is in piercing clarity.
All I remember is that silver stud,
and that it hurt like hell
when he pierced me.

Sarah Blakely

Ink

These memories are permanent ink
injected into my body and brain
like the tattoos that cover your skin.
But the lines have blurred over time,
your features are faded and worn.
Some days your face is clear as ever,
behind those glaring glinting glasses,
staring straight back at me.
Other days I fail to recall your image,
resembling a dark shadowy splotch of ink,
bleeding into every limb.

When Your Body Remembers
But Your Brain Does Not

I may not remember
why the taste of piña coladas
grows sour in my mouth.
I may not remember
who it was or when or where
he forced himself on me.
But my body remembers,
as the drink goes down,
let the anxiety sink in.
Fruity and sweet,
it quickens my heartbeat,
but time passes so slowly.
Twitching echoes of bodily screams,
reverberating trauma
underneath my skin.
Each jolt of lightning
attempting to illuminate
dark ink blots on my brain.
There's a spot on the X-ray
where this memory was,
a missing puzzle piece.

Sarah Blakely

It must've fallen into the cracks
of my broken glass memories,
sharp shards ready to slice me up.

Lost Memories

Memories disguised,
undetected, unrecognized.
My brain frantically tries
decoding what the image implies -
much to my surprise,
these distant stories aren't lies.
I purge the tears from my eyes,
wondering if it's okay to cry,
or should I quietly agonize
over the dim vision of moonrise.
Sometimes it's myself I despise,
when it's easy to over-analyze
faded scars on pale thighs
as the little girl within me dies.

Sarah Blakely

Mining For Memories

Grab a shovel, grab your pick,
don't forget your helmet!
Watch for falling fragments of rocks as we
go mining for gemstone memories.
Deep underground can be dangerous
while we hammer and chisel the rough,
but then looky here!
Some colors appear,
this must be the mineral memory I've been
    searching for
now I'm hooked on my healing, I need to
    find more.

The Past

I am not my past,
but the past is all I'll ever be.
I wonder if a part of you ever
fell in love with a past version of me.

If I am not my past,
but the past is where they always leave me,
dreading my past, cursing trauma,
I wonder how the future will see me.

I am not my past,
but the past is always behind me,
creeping up in the building shadows,
the past is always there to remind me.

A Motel Haunting

Something about your friend's apartment
reminded me of the motel from long ago
where my body was stolen from me,
ripped out of my hands so violently.

Something about its proximity to the
    7-Eleven,
or the way the streetlight hits the night sky
    air,
sounds of a busy street, pedestrians unaware
of crimes committed within these
    floral walls.

Small Hands

He laughed and said I have small hands,
pressing his massive palm up to mine.

The image of our hands clasped together
threw me back in time ten years

to when *he* laughed and said I have small
        hands,
pressing his massive palm up to mine.

Sarah Blakely

I Forgot To Bury My Body
When He Killed Me

I lie awake in bed at night
listening to the moaning wind.
It must've had a nightmare too,
a flashback of a cold dark sky,
biting quietly at my neck,
heartbeats race like shooting stars.
It's nearing the anniversary of my death,
but there was never a proper burial.
Every year, my spirit comes back to haunt.
The drowning sadness, impulsive restlessness,
and suspicious motives to top it off.
Not this season.
I'll condemn the spirit as I should've
the night my pure constellation faded.

This Halloween I Am Going To Be Re-Traumatized

It is October and the trees are all scab and
          bruise,
stirring up these feelings like some evil
          witches brew.
Poisonous thoughts infecting my brain,
pomegranate lipstick leaving a stain,
the moaning trees sound just like screams
of scarecrows ripping right through their
          seams,
hard apple cider gone bittersweet,
you were the trick, I was the treat.

And now there are ghosts that wander this
          hall,
reappearing in nightmares every fall,
the weight of you is crushing me,
the way your skin felt almost scaley,
like some monster in the night,
an evil creature, a horrifying sight.
You've crawled inside me, like a demon,
I've been possessed and you're the reason.

Dearly Departed

I look in the mirror and see a ghost,
an apparition of my younger self,
phantom flashbacks of my past
echoing in my hollow skull.
October is always dark nights
filled with frights and candle light,
holding a seance with all my lost memories,
retrieving what fragments I can through
       the veil.

Deep in my bones, I know
the scariest image in my head
is midnight in a hotel room
dancing with demons in disguise,
moaning like the wind,
"good girl."
Skeletons and secrets rest eternally
in this graveyard of memories.

Christmas Ghost

He haunts my arctic mind
like a ghost of Christmas past,
tormenting my frozen December fingers,
balled up in snowy white fists,
forever fighting off his memory.
It's as effective as punching a phantom.

Twitch

Drive, talk.
Listen, laugh.
Stop, talk.
Listen, laugh.
Move, flinch.
Laugh, tease.
Touch, twitch.
Wonder, why?
Calm, hug.
Worry, why?
Hug, kiss.
Touch, flinch.
Ask, nothing.
Worry, wonder.
Later, later.
Tease, touch.
Hug, kiss.
Smile.
No twitch.

Eruption

Rumbling, bubbling, glowing,
red hot embering magma
gurgles underneath my solid shield.
My heartbeat tremors temperamentally,
triggering a terrible traumatic temper
tantrum of tectonic destruction.
Catapulting combustion,
creating a cavernous crater,
angry lava emerges from the devil's depths,
an inferno of fiery hellish rage.
Ash falls cloaking the clouded sky,
choking and charring my lungs,
a poisonous plume of panic.
Metamorphosing my dormant heart
into sharp, shattering obsidian glass.

Sarah Blakely

You Turned Me Into A Disaster Scene

originally published by ZIMETRA magazine

Our favorite rock band plays through my
      headphones
and suddenly something is moving,
breaking underneath my surface.

I'm straddling an active fault
and your memory is the hypocenter
buried miles below my mantle.

My body starts to tremble,
I feel the magnitude of this quake
deep in my bones, to my core.

Tectonic plates shifting inside me,
seismic activity below my skin,
my heart rate spikes as the pressure rises.

Shaking at high velocity now,
tsunami waves pouring out of my eyes,
I'm stuck in this Ring of Fire that is my rage.

For a moment, my blood is magma
and my chest feels like it's collapsing
like the cathedral in Christchurch in 2011.

That same year you put your hands on me
for the first time, because in the aftermath,
devastation is what friends are for.

They say aftershocks can be just as deadly,
just as severe as the time you tore me down
like tumbling bricks crashing, my knees
        hitting the sidewalk.

They say this is all just normal stress,
that the up-and-down rhythm of your body
        on mine
is just a natural frequency and not a
        traumatic event.

Your collision into me caused such
        subduction
that I've created an oceanic trench, a severe
        depression,
and I've crawled to the bottom to hide from
        this destruction.

Sarah Blakely

That Song By Pendulum Still Makes Me Want To Scream

I'm safe now,
yet I still hear your voice
whispering in my ear
telling me I'm worthless,
that I'm yours to degrade
and no one else can have me.

I'm safe now,
yet I still worry
you'll show up at my door
in the middle of the night,
hunting me down again,
stalking me like your prey.

I'm safe now,
yet I still am afraid
to wake the neighbors
with my screams,
I know all too well
that nobody will save me.

By The End Of May, I Fall Apart

Memorial Day weekend of 2009
echoes in my body, twisting in my mind,
a vine, I'm entwined, wrapped in my past.
Make a beeline for the wine,
my body is not mine,
and I'm not doing fine.
Why can't I just enjoy the sunshine,
why can't my life have a normal storyline,
without abuse on my mind
like all of the damn time.
Write it down, get it out,
but it still haunts me at night,
all these battles I fight,
invisible wounds brought to light.
It's a grisly sight, feel free to leave if you like,
or you could just hold me real tight
and tell me that I'll be alright.

Grieving Childhood Abuse

My brain grieves the loss of my memory,
education I worked hard to attain.
My transcripts reflect when my mental
      health
mutated to shit and flushed down the drain.

My body grieves the loss of my innocence,
transformed into a woman too young.
My bruises reveal the decade of damage
caused by his hand as it swung.

My soul grieves the loss of my inner child,
banished to hide away in the dark.
My voice resonates through the hollow hole
in my throat where he left his mark.

December Always Slaps A Label On Me For The New Year

It happened in December.
On a cold metal bench
in a park along the bike path,
right by the creek,
after the road curves.
Victim.

It happened in December.
In the University health center
on a sterile doctor's office table
right across the hall from the pharmacy,
my next stop on this tour.
Traumatized.

It happened in December.
In a cushioned ugly chair
at the psychiatrist's office downtown,
right as my brain
began to spin.
Crazy.

Drinking Poison

Some days,
the doubts and criticism
get so bad,
it's like drinking poison.
But it goes down so smoothly,
clouding my mental sky,
a sickness of the head.

Powder

Feeling powerful in powdered
amber golds and matte
raspberry cream.

I wish I felt this
mighty in
my own skin.

62

Tainted Love

64

Chess

He played me
like a game of chess.
I thought I was the Queen,
but I was only his pawn.

Sarah Blakely

What Kind Of Man

He kisses me with his fist,
apologizes for treating me like this.
But he never changes his ways,
he leaves bruises that stay.

What kind of man loves like this?

Depression Is A Serial Killer

I've been left with bruises on my face
and bleeding from inside,
how can I trade in all this pain
for a happy ending guide?

I need instructions, be specific,
on how to keep the good alive.
I always seem to crush or kill it,
with me, depression is the vibe.

Seventeen

I survived being seventeen.

In the span of one year,
I was raped four times
by four different men,
dumped by the man I thought I loved
(for being raped),
lost my first job to the trauma,
and lost my grandpa to the reaper.

I was suicidal most of the year,
morbid curiosity consumed me.

And then there was you.
You gave me hope,
you gave me love,
you gave me kindness,

and I gave you up.

I could've crumbled,
I could've admitted defeat.
But I overcame.
And I attribute my triumph
partially to you.

Sarah Blakely

Being Your Girlfriend Did Not Make It Okay

It started out as sweet
as the flowers you presented me,
bursting from our friend's red PT cruiser
after chasing my bus ten miles to town.

"Call Me Maybe" played on the radio,
you made up our own little chorus,
"Hey, I just met you, and this is crazy,
but here's some flowers, please be my
        girlfriend!"

I said yes that time,
but later down the line
you heard me say no,
yet you made me do it anyway.

Don't Tell Me To Leave The Past Behind

They say to leave the dead to die,
leave their blood in the streets,
but I'm the girl collecting the bones
after the dogs have devoured the meat.

I can't let go of these pieces of you,
even the daggers of broken shards,
can't bring myself to burn your memory,
or lay your remains in the graveyard.

Someday perhaps I'll put you to rest,
but for now, I want you to stay,
so I'll keep you in my heart's collection
of long-lost lovers left to decay.

Alex

I'll never forget
how you made me breakfast,
listened to me cry,
and drove me back home
the morning after
he raped me.

He Must've Missed The Battle Scene

"I'm happy to hear about your successes,"
he said as he hugged me goodbye.
He makes it seem like I haven't been
      suffering
alone for so many years, recovering from
      trauma
rather slowly, somewhat reluctantly.

He makes it seem like I haven't been facing
mental health monsters, with nothing
protecting me but a tin shield of hope.
Nothing to fight back with but a tiny
      toothpick,
against this venomous hydra in my mind.

I'm training for the trauma Olympics,
confronting corrupt memories,
going to war equipped with words I didn't
      have before.
"Stop," and "no," meant nothing back then.
I've since strengthened my vocal cords,
learned to project.

Sarah Blakely

I realize now that I don't think he knows
what happened to me as a child.
He's been there for it all, but a minor
        character,
behind the scenes, curtain dropped,
while the battles raged on across my stage.

When The Feminist Falls For The Alpha Male

Every day I'm more bitter,
craving what I can't have with you.
Logically, I know we'd set each other on fire,
carcinogens leaking from burnt love letters,
toxic romance polluting the air.
Yet still, I desire the warmth
of your body next to mine,
nevermind if it burns me up in my sleep.
I still think about that time we had sex
after I told you about my history of abuse,
and you said you felt like you were *raping* me.
Such an odd thing to say,
coming from a man I trusted.
(But then again, aren't we all raped
by men we thought we could trust?)
I should've known
when you said you were an alpha male,
there was no question in your desire to
        dominate.
Even in your desire to dominate me.

My Truth

My truth is I've never had a healthy
     relationship.
My truth is trauma is all I know.
I wish I could say that wasn't the case,
I wish I could let it all go.

Heartache and loneliness haunt me,
echoing anxiety and insecurities in my head.
I'd never survive the winter
if I listened to what some of them said.

They scream all the names men have
     called me
in anger or lusty pursuit,
they tell me I should pull the trigger,
but I don't have the will to shoot.

I keep on wanting to believe
there's someone out there for me,
someone who can hold me as I cry,
someone who truly sees me for me.

But the good ones never seem to know
quite how to handle my damage,
they start out hopeful they can heal me,
but it always ends up being too much to
        manage.

I'm terrified you'll change your mind
        about us,
I've been harboring so much doubt.
Maybe the only way to be happy
is to not let the truth come out.

Leave A Scar

We say we're not addicted,
but these industries have tricked us
into reading all that's printed
and believing in the power of lipstick,
but a woman is so much more
than the sex of which she is born.
We move on when we get bored
and we show them no remorse.

What kind of girl am I to say no to a man?
What kind of misled fool would offer me
        their hand?
And I'm still trying to understand
why a woman like me even wants a man
when all they give me is a broken heart
and a series of blows to leave a scar,
I know you'll just leave a scar.

I'm a hopeless romantic but I'm not boy
crazy,
I won't fall for a guy just cuz he says he's in
the Navy.

But I'll admit when I'm hit, my vision gets
    a little hazy,
and when that special someone is around,
    no doubt I'm shaking.
I just want to feel your soft skin,
and the thought of it makes me cringe.
While I really do want to find my prince,
there's a war of emotions raging within.

And I can say that I don't want it,
but I can't say it's always true,
I'm kind of tired of all things platonic
when all I want to be is with you,
I just wanna be with you.

What kind of girl am I to say no to a man?
What kind of misled fool would offer me
    their hand?
And I'm still trying to understand
why a woman like me even wants a man
when all they give me is a broken heart
and a series of blows to leave a scar,
I know you'll just leave a scar.

This one is mine for the taking
but he'll just leave me breaking,
I think about all the time I'm wasting
looking for something that's so degrading
but it's also so breathtaking
and my body is aching,
I just want somebody to love
but why can't I just be enough?
I keep finding myself in a rush
just to find somebody I trust,
so I settle for their lust
and all they do is thrust into me,
I got a bit of a crush,
but all they do is thrust into me.

Fingerprints

He left his fingerprints
in blood around my neck,
and I'm sorry, love,
for every time you reach your hand
sensually around my throat,
I fear you'll smear those crimson marks.
I wish I could swallow
these memories he left,
but they have such sharp edges,
they'd slice me from inside.

Sarah Blakely

You Ask Me To Pick A Card
And I Draw My Swords

I'm hoping that when the cards fall,
they fall in our favor,
but my hand seems to keep drawing swords,
begging for blood and violence.

Call it muscle memory,
call it having a flashback in bed,
I'm always reaching for daggers,
I can't sleep in this peaceful silence.

Nightmares stabbing into my slumber,
slicing into my dreams,
healing feels a lot like carving myself up,
my body as a jack o' lantern.

Take these knives away from me,
no bloodshed in this bed.
The only crimes committed here
should be crimes of love and passion.

Good Girl

He says "good girl"
as if it's a good thing.
As if those words
were never used as a gun to my head.
As if being a good girl
has ever made me any less victim.
I wipe the shame from my face,
continuing to playfully kiss his fingertips.
My shoulder twitches and I hope he doesn't
        notice,
but he notices, he stops, and holds me close.
My love overcomes the fear.

Sarah Blakely

Flawed Fruit

I wonder if he sees the subtle scars
intertwined with the ink on my thighs.
When his fingers trace my tattoo,
I wonder if he senses the damage I'm
            trying to disguise.

Bruises on my cheek left by other men,
dissolved quietly into my skin,
but they've left their mark on my memory,
residual pain echoes within.

I'm still in disbelief at times
that he picked me from the tree,
flawed fruit, battered and blemished,
I wonder if I taste as sweet.

Ask Me What I Like
originally published by Querencia Press

When a man asks me
what I like in bed,
I tend to tell him
what he wants to hear.

That I am dirty,
filthy from being
repeatedly shoved into the ground
face-first.

I like it rough,
like the jagged edges
of shattered glass,
because I am broken.

I want to feel his machismo,
beating into my body
like the gavel that decided
I am not worthy of justice.

Like the hammer and nail
that boarded up my heart,
trapping me inside my own body,
an animal with no way out.

Sarah Blakely

When a man asks me
what I really like,
I will tell him honestly.
I'm not sure.

I like the feeling
of lips meeting,
introducing themselves sweetly
like the sun gently rising in the morning.

I like tender touching,
carefully caressing,
playfully pawing,
when fingers feel like feathers on my skin.

I like palms pressed together
perceiving the pulsing,
the pleasure and excitement
of studying your rhythmic love.

I like knowing
my body is safe,
but I rarely find a man
who is shield instead of spear.

Boa Constrictor Boys

Papery snake skin sheds
draped over blades of grass
in the summer garden.
Lessons in evolution,
I collected them in jars.

That same summer,
I invited a boa constrictor
into bed with me.
He wrapped himself around my body,
smothering me in my sleep.

Every night,
I made room for him
in bed,
as he made room for me
in his stomach.

Feminine Rage

The Caged Singer

I take so much pride in my voice
but when I'm not heard
I'm about as effective as a caged bird.

Sarah Blakely

Screaming At The Luminaries

Hit me with the
sun's joy rays
like a spade
over my head.

Hit me with the
deep moonlight
like a knife
into my chest.

I can't take their
hopeful glow
when I know
all they witness.

I can't take their
daily route,
while I shout
they hear nothing.

Screaming at the
sun and moon,
they're immune
to my temper.

Victim Blaming

I drank too much.
I didn't fight back.
I didn't say no
when he attacked.
I wore cute clothes.
I painted a target.
I didn't carry a weapon
of defense in my pocket.
I didn't dare tell him
that I was afraid.
My throat closed up,
my silence betrayed me.
Can you call it a moan
if it was made in pain?
These are the thoughts
that haunt my brain.

Blame Me

Of course, it was *my* fault.
It was *my* fault your boyfriend cheated.
Because clearly boys can't be trusted.
Even when you love them.
Even when they say you're the only one.
Why is it that I was the one that was
lectured by *his* mom,
yelled at by *his* girlfriend,
and sneered at in the halls?
While he went on dating her,
free of any punishment.
Now I remember,
boys never get blamed.

Accountability

My name is accountability,
and I'm coming for you.
You who can't be bothered to remember
      my name,
substituting with common labels - "her",
    "girl", "lady".
You who spew insensitive drunken rape jokes
in the immediate presence of a survivor.
You who refuse to apologize because your
      belief is the only truth -
she *obviously* wanted it.
You who take and take and take, and never
      offer sacrifice in return,
never offer anything meaningful, worthwhile,
      or valuable.
Take me, take my body, rip it up, and spit on
      my shredded paper skin -
take it all, it's your birthright as the white
      man.
I will rise and come back to haunt you,
you won't get away with these offenses.

Sarah Blakely

I Didn't Ask For It

I didn't ask for this body.
I recoiled from its curves,
felt disgusting in dresses,
shorts, skirts, anything that showed skin.
I hid in hoodies for ten whole years.

I didn't ask for their hunger.
I said no to their wanting,
but they took bites of me anyway,
pieces of my body are still branded with
      their initials.
I became a prized steer and everyone wanted
      to slaughter me.

Twelve

If tomorrow, I were healed,
I'd use today to shout.
To stomp and yell,
throw a tantrum,
because hell,
I was only twelve.

The child in me never had her day
to cry and scream,
to feel this way.
And she deserves it, dammit.

She deserves to be living life
at twenty-seven,
without a lifetime of therapy sessions,
she deserves to travel and meet new people
and not wonder if they're secretly evil
and going to hurt her if she lets her guard
      down
or trample around in her sacred garden.

Sarah Blakely

She deserves to flutter free with joy,
spread her wings, not her legs,
a butterfly,
like the ones she painted in art class
before you broke through the glass
and she understood what it meant
when the radio DJ said she sounded hot –

at age twelve.

Before she'd wonder forever
if he knew or could tell,
or maybe could smell her youth
through the phone line
requesting her favorite song by MCR
which is oddly enough
about the death of a girl
at the hands of a man,

(I should've known there would be
some meaning to that)

and before she thinks, or rather, knows
that men are sharks with a keen nose
for pubescent girls, and vicious teeth
to rip them up from underneath
it's just our species, human nature
to kill and take, pillage and rape.

She learned a lot in middle school
through the actions of men,
yet she became the fool,
she grew up too fast.

So now I need to make it last.

Sarah Blakely

Like Taking Kandi From A Baby

Maybe I should've been studying algebra,
instead of copying down lyrics in my
          journals
written by tattooed men twice my age,
aggressively screaming into a microphone
about old high school girlfriends
they wish they'd killed,
and collecting bras from preteen fans
turned violated victims of this predatory
          scene.

How can we escape the fate we were dealt?
A hand full of jokers in guyliner
with pierced lips begging to tear me up
          with a kiss,
holding guitars with more care
than the hearts of sad girls they cruelly
          crushed.
And we had to be sad,
or else we weren't precious enough,
not special enough to write a song about.

They molded us into starving junior models
with skin-tight plastic beaded bracelets
to cover up the cuts on our wrists,
and heavy raccoon eyeliner
just so they could watch it run
down our faces as we cried.
The fallen angel, the damaged damsel,
the manic pixie dream girl, it's all a lie.

I remember my first concert when I was
        thirteen,
full of young girls just like me, frienemies
pitted against each other in a fight to the
        death,
crushing rib cages while swarming the pit,
screaming and squawking like shrieking birds
all fighting over the worms on stage,
worms much bigger than us, and looking
        back,
I think they might've been snakes.

Sarah Blakely

Patterns Of Abuse

She said,
"I'm seeing a pattern here."
As if me being raped
is a bad habit I have,
a self-destructive ritual,
a sick routine,
a shameful tradition.
As if my clothes
or my perfume
or my behavior
or anything other than
the rapists who raped me
were to blame.

Good Guys Don't Rape People

"He's such a good guy though!"
That's what they always say,
and it drives me insane.
Do they think I'm imagining this pain?

Because you didn't feel his grip on my wrist,
or hear how he called me a bitch
when I refused to kiss his lips,
you didn't see me resist, so the struggle
        didn't exist.

Are you saying it's okay
that he tried to have his way
while my unconscious body lay?
What about that situation is gray?

Just because he's your friend
doesn't mean you have to defend
every action of his until the end.
Is it really that easy to play pretend?

Everyone knows a survivor
but as soon as they inquire
they're likely to call her a liar
or say that she liked having him inside her.

And nobody blames the violence
on the ones who forced us into silence,
to keep our voices from spreading like
          a virus,
as if the truth being known is the crisis.

It happens again and again,
men choose rapists as their friends,
paying no mind to how we've bled
at the hands of their buddies in this
          vicious trend.

Power Hungry

I'm scrolling Facebook,
stumble upon someone I may know.
Him.

The pot simmers.

Adrenaline rushes after almost 8 years
        dormant,
seeing that same stone-cold face,
rugged and beastly.
Even worse,
holding assault weapons.

The pot bubbles hot.

I never knew he was in the army,
I never knew his birthday, how old he was,
I never knew his last name.
He was a rough and terrifying gargoyle
        of a man,
muscular in the way that makes you feel
        powerless.

The pot boils.

Power.
Some men join the military
to feel power.
All rape is about power.

Some Men Are Snakes And They Hide In Broad Daylight

I'm tired of these reptilian men
hiding under rocks
disguised as your friends,
and when I tell you the truth,
you deny and defend
their so-called "honor,"
insisting on their innocence.
He sunk his fangs into my neck,
make no mistake, he had intent,
but it doesn't matter to you,
covering your ears to my lament,
ignoring my wounds
unless there's proof I can document.
Does my memory count?
Is my voice enough evidence?
Don't you trust me at all?
Or is our friendship pretend?

F Is For Friends

A handful of acquaintances from high
    school.
A guy I used to make out with in secret.
A friend's older brother who I've met
    maybe once.
My ex's dad who I've actually met once.
A neighbor from around the corner.
A girl I used to take the bus to school with.
A friend's mom, entirely a stranger.
Some familiar faces I've seen around town.
A man who raped me in college, zero
    mutual friends.
A guy who assaulted me in high school,
we have 14 mutual friends
who don't believe me.

The Self-Proclaimed Nice Guy
originally published by Querencia Press

He's saying I'm being a bitch
but what did I do to deserve this?
Is it because I said "no"?
He's got to learn how to let go.

He calls himself a nice guy
as he complains and wonders why
none of the girls want to talk to him
while he's quietly stalking them.

He says to let him explain
but I don't want to entertain
his bad behavior and sad excuses,
why can't he just accept when a woman
        refuses?

Suddenly I'm afraid for my life
as he approaches my house with a knife,
and it will be my fault for not knowing
        self-defense.
How the hell does that make any sense?

Sarah Blakely

It's a crime in itself how often we women
are threatened to be turned into shades
          of crimson,
streaks on the sidewalk, police walk over
          this violence
because it's not a crime scene until
          someone's lying lifeless.

Define Bad

Would you rather read a story
with a violent ending?
Would you rather read the headline
containing a woman's murder?
Just because we deal with bad behavior
      every day
doesn't make it okay
for men to stalk us like prey,
and then simply laugh and say
that "nothing bad actually happened."

Sarah Blakely

Standing Too Close To The Sun

He stood right in front of me,
blocking my vision, closing me off,
in the claustrophobic corner of this
already-cramped rest stop McDonald's.

I sidestepped twice
to give room for his forcefield
of all-consuming maleness.
And twice, he eclipsed me,
turning me to shadows,
while his oblivious solar flares
burned my pale lunar skin as he passed.

Men are always the biggest,
brightest star in their solar system.
But only the moon recognizes
the tyranny of their blazing beams.
The sun takes up so much space,
ignorant and unaware
of its destructive role,
incinerating any celestial bodies
within arms reach.

Lavender Lattes

Carefully crafting
criminally caffeinated coffee
consumed in chocolate raspberry
laced kisses.
Call her your lover, or rather,
your libation,
pouring seductive shots
of roses and honey,
aromas to intoxicate the senses.
Your lavender lattes
taste like distrust,
malicious mint mochas
served to a feminine demographic,
violated by exotic vanilla beans,
bad manners brewing in the back room.

Sarah Blakely

Every School Has Its Skeletons

The scariest part about leaving for college
is that you might come back a corpse
rather than a graduate.
The near-ancient buildings are haunted
by the horrible happenings of campus life
resulting in student death.
Girls turned ghosts before becoming women,
boys to beastly animals, packs of wolves
in fraternity houses.
This week, they found a human skeleton
on a California college campus
hidden away in an isolated residential hall.
I wonder how long they'd been there.
Dusty and dead, spirit and bones,
dwelling in lonely shadows.

I Left University Because

It felt more like a victims closet,
with limp skeletons hanging from men's
        fingers,
bones heavier than textbooks.
It felt more like a graveyard,
I became a ghost on that campus,
grieving the loss of my body to a man's knife.

I remember walking to the library one day,
seeing thousands of little flags planted in
        the earth,
a quiet memorial service to all the dead
        women
still roaming those halls,
solemnly searching for peace.
I stood in silence, wanting to cry.

Nobody in my poetry class wanted to
        discuss my poems,
they were too heavy, too uncomfortable.
Imagine being the one who lives inside
        these words.

Sarah Blakely

To my female peers, I was brave,
but to the boys in my class, I was just another
          big mouth,
a throat to choke, to strangle into silence.

My rapist was allowed to stay at school,
a murderer disguised as a student.
I lost faith in higher education when I
          realized,
it didn't matter how hard I studied,
they would rather keep his tuition money
than keep women safe.

Lessons On Selling Sugar

Nobody had to teach me
how to sell sugar.
Nobody needed to explain
that men have an insatiable sweet tooth,
tongues tracing lollipop lips,
between tantric trembling hips.
It was the unspoken rule,
if I exposed my candy,
there will always be an audience
willing to pay for a taste.

Sarah Blakely

Song For A Sex Worker

You'd never suspect her,
in this turtleneck,
to be a good girl
with a bad sex complex.
Cover up the purple
marks on her neck,
just one of many side effects
of sleeping with a man
for a damn paycheck.

He gives her just enough respect
for a damaged sex object,
he calls her cute in this skirt
but she's an absolute wreck,
acts like a brute in pursuit
of degrading sex,
it's no flex,
can't forget the latex
cuz she's dirty the way he likes it,
spreading her pollution
with legs wide open.

Substitute his wedding ring
for some rubber thing,
she's a last resort,
he fucks her for sport,
behind secret meetings, closed doors,
he says he can't afford a divorce.
Strip her down
to her birthday suit,
he stares in awe,
his body salutes.

Sarah Blakely

Don't Come For Me
originally published by Querencia Press

If we as women
are the genuine majority,
why do uptight white men
still claim authority
over our bodies,
our right to choose?
Because in reality,
we're the ones with everything to lose
when our bodily rights
are on the line,
and suddenly my body
feels less mine.

The way a man wants
to fertilize me,
staring at me like
I'm a piece of prize meat,
even when he's my lover
and I tell him no,
he takes it personally,
calls me a hoe.

But he doesn't recognize
that it's not about him,
because for me, it's a bodily process,
not just a whim.
He says he wants a child now
but where will he be once it arrives?
It should be the woman's decision
if she wants to survive.

I can't put a face
to the man that angers me most,
but I know it's a man
turning me into a ghost,
torturing, raping,
demanding control
of my body, mind
and my impure soul,
burning me at the stake
like my grandmothers before me,
it takes on a new meaning now
when they say they're coming for me.

Sarah Blakely

I Must Be The Treasury For His Family Jewels

Womb of a woman,
built to breed bloodlines,
to be fertile with fear,
to generate and incubate.

Birthing heirs
who will assume this throne
before my reign is over,
before I even let my seat get cold.

I'm the keeper of the family crypt,
but the names on these tombstones
all belong to men
claiming the right to my existence.

The walls of my uterus
like a vault at a museum,
holding all my king's riches
inside.

Abortion Should Not Be A Synonym For Danger

originally published by Querencia Press

When an ultrasound reveals small signs of
        unborn life,
why is my full-grown body
suddenly secondary?

Why am I an outlaw, a refugee,
my right to choose –
unconstitutional?

Why am I reminded of blood,
gushing crimson, and pain,
the result of a back alley operation?

Why are old white men in stuffy suits
still in control of my body,
restricting my reproductive rights?

Why do they care so much
if there's a heartbeat in my uterus,
are they forgetting about the one beating
        in my chest?

Sarah Blakely

Why does it feel like being
raped, being unsafe,
all because my womanhood is a fucking
debate?

Shut Me Up

Men are always trying to shut me up.
Whether it's my moans of pleasure or
        screams of pain,
they cover my mouth, bind me and gag me,
as if they're trying their best to contain
this beast of a woman, this monstrous
        maiden,
this soulful siren song driving them insane.
How dare they try to silence my power,
I will not be tamed nor chained,
while they run their mouths at me
and rudely try to mansplain
why I belong in a darkened dungeon
so that they can easier abstain
from fondling and fucking me,
as if my body's beauty needs to be
        restrained
when they're the ones in reality
acting so crude and profane.

Sarah Blakely

I Fight Like A Woman
originally published by Querencia Press

"You should probably carry pepper spray."
Concern is what he was trying to convey.
Though all I heard was the voice of this
      system,
you should try to be less of a victim.

What about the ones victimizing?
How come nobody's criticizing
their horrible actions, violations?
It seems all they see is the fixation.

It must be women's work to defend their
      bodies
against beastly men making rape a hobby.
We don't get badges for valor or glory,
we're rewarded for how well we hide our
      fury.

I laugh it off, knowing he doesn't
    understand,
I've gripped a can of mace like a lover's
    hand,
I don't leave without it, hold it closer at
    night,
he'll never know how we women have to
    fight.

Sarah Blakely

How Long Must Women Wait

How long must women wait for liberty?
For autonomy over our bodies and minds.
Freedom to declare what's ours as our own.
To be the ruler of our own worlds,
queens of our own queendoms.

How long must women wait for recovery?
We as women are natural healers,
we reconstruct ourselves like damaged
      starfish,
torn limb from limb by degenerate predators,
disfiguring our bodies for sheer pleasure.

How long must women wait for justice?
In a system that heckles those with courage,
choosing to report their abuser.
A system that (occasionally) finds men
      guilty of vile crimes,
yet sets them free with a slap on the wrist.

How long must women wait for answers?
How will leaders face this epidemic called
    rape?
What will they do to protect us?
Why don't they take us seriously?
When will the world serve us equally?

Kitchen Bitch

For a woman, knives belong in the kitchen
or in the backs of other women.
All the whores and bitches
running their mouths
instead of running to get groceries,
to feed the hungry mouths of helpless men
who never learned to cut vegetables
yet they can wield a knife and threaten a life
as if it's second nature.

For a woman, hunger isn't just for food,
but for power, equality, and justice.
We crave the day we can walk freely
without simmering rage,
bubbling and boiling over
at every man we come across, coyotes,
yipping and yelling, telling us to smile,
threatening vile acts if we don't obey.
Obedience is a means of survival.

For a woman, anger is the fire on the stove,
controlled, tame, caged in.
It is the fuel that keeps us going,
but has the potential to burn our tongues,
scorching us from the inside out
as we swallow it down in silence.
We keep our anger in the kitchen,
as men feast in dining rooms designed for
        misogyny.
I think it's time the woman gets a seat at
        the table.

Sarah Blakely

Sex Education Is A Lot Like Home Economics

I always wondered how the penis
would end up inside the vagina
in the first place.
I never asked my teacher about this,
afraid of being laughed at
for not knowing my place.

As if women are all homemakers,
making a home for a man
inside our own bodies.
Push-up bras, fluffing pillows,
they always find a way
to get comfortable in our bodies.

Of all these things I learned,
I was never taught
how to be safe.
So when he laughed at me
for trying to put on a condom upside-down,
asking, "don't you know how to be safe?"

I shook my head, no,
men have always
made that choice for me.

Sarah Blakely

Eggs

In sixth grade,
they began teaching us
about sex, all sperm and eggs.
Then in seventh,
they threw in
home economics.

In sex ed,
they taught us
how an egg gets fertilized.
In home ec,
they taught us
how to cook an egg.

I learned in eighth grade
it would always be me
on the menu.
Sunny-side up,
scrambled,
doesn't matter.

Conquerors

I've taken back my body
from these violent conquerors.
I've worked hard to nurture it,
cultivate this soil.

It's finally mine again,
after being claimed as property
by men jabbing their flags into my earth,
into places they were never invited.

It's *finally* mine again,
and you tell me the clock is ticking,
surrender, wave the white flag,
so you can steal me away from myself,

peel my skin from the bone,
take what is left and sacrifice it
in the name of your god,
in the name of your unborn child.

Sarah Blakely

Girls Gone Feral
originally published by Querencia Press

Girls gone feral
after domestication
by men who want a
woman clean-shaven,
to give up her body
as a humble donation.

Girls gone feral
demand an amputation
from men who want a
pretty conversation
to last longer than their
sexual duration.

Girls gone feral
want domination
of men who want a
woman's sensation,
dripping and needy,
feels like holy salvation.

Girls gone feral
cause agitation
in men who want a
woman's admiration,
craving that helpless
look of adoration.

Girls gone feral
learn flirtation
with men who want a
physical confrontation,
turning aggression
into an excavation.

Girls gone feral
have a reputation
towards men who want a
woman's devastation,
but these women
have no obligation.

Sarah Blakely

Girls gone feral
evoke temptation
in men who want a
kingly coronation
while developing a dark
rape culture fixation.

Furor Uterinus
originally published by Querencia Press

Oh, the fury.

The fury of the womb,
and what it means to carry one inside
        of you.
The fury of femaleness,
cold biological names for what I am,
for the anger I hold,
woven into my mitochondrial DNA,
anger towards men who have never been
and will never be
a woman.

Oh, the madness.

The madness of menstruation,
that monthly reminder that pain is a part
        of life.
The blood and blame,
staining names and hands red,
guilty of imagined crimes,
conjuring up spectral evidence,
imagining murder and sin and devil worship,
but why would I worship
a man?

Sarah Blakely

Liminal Spaces
originally published by Querencia Press

I'm in between a B cup and a C.
The gap between my thighs
(but there is no gap, I lied),
the dent in my forehead
between my eyes,
the valley between my breasts,
where my heart hides in its cage.

I'm in between couch cushions,
the void, vortex, vagina,
something vague, vaporous,
a spirit between worlds
disappearing at any moment.

I'm in between first kiss and
the hundredth set of lips,
the window where my front teeth
peek from behind soft pink flesh
between a reaching cupid's bow
and vermillion border.

I'm in between menarche,
(first menstruation for those
who need better sex education)
and some hundredth ovulation,
but how many chances do I get
at creation?

I'm in between virgin and mother,
no stranger to men and coarse hands
cause me to suffer, suffocating
when they should be supplementing
my feminine force.

I'm in between tame and feral,
wild and unclaimed,
something terrible.

I'm not a girl, not yet a woman.

Sarah Blakely

A Woman's No
after "The Lady's Yes" by Elizabeth Barrett Browning
originally published by Querencia Press

"No" should be the red light
at a busy intersection.
It should stop them in their tracks,
if only it were such a simple rejection.

Saying no should be taught in school
as well as the proper response to the word
because it seems these days to deny a man
is a sin, and so my "no" is never heard.

It's not that it is not spoken though,
but a two-letter word puts up no fight
against a man in lusty pursuit,
so we've got to teach them to behave at
          night.

When a woman says "no," you can be sure
she knows just what she's saying
and if you wanted to do right by her
you'd be listening and obeying.

Withdraw your greedy grabbing hand
and offer your heart instead,
show her she can trust you,
show her how you've bled.

Don't pester or jest until she says yes,
because that's not a yes to her,
and a yes while under influence
is nothing more than a blur.

"No" can come in many forms
and many small details,
ignore them and you may find yourself
rotting away in jail.

Learning Survival

Healing Takes Time

I remember the sun
walking out of
the court hall that day.

It blinded me with joy
finished at last
but I wasn't done.

Healing is a long road
coiled and cloudy
it takes a long time.

I'm still healing, hurting,
but I'll get there
one day I'll be free.

Sarah Blakely

10 Of Wands Reversed

Unburden yourself
from the baggage
filled with trauma
you've been carrying
around on your back
for so long.

Put down your damage,
drop your weapons,
no need for self-defense.
Not anymore.
You are safe.
You are whole.

I Am Sturdy As An Old Oak Tree

They say without the wind,
young trees would not develop strength.
But the wind is a gentle breeze most days.
He was a raging tempest,
hurling bolts of lightning
at my bark and branches.
He left scorch mark scars in my trunk,
but the sap that leaks from these wounds
is proof of life, prevailing.

Sarah Blakely

Fossil

When my fossilized skeleton
is unearthed someday,
a relic of an earlier civilization,
I wonder if those who study my bones
will see my trauma
imprinted on my body
like the rings in the trunk of a tree,
and if they'll be able to measure
the weight of the damage it caused,
or the inner strength it took
to survive.

Blooming

We are limbs,
bent and coiled
in misshapen forms,
a knotted tree trunk
leaning to one side
in this cruel garden.

Twisted, but blooming.

Water my roots,
needy and bare,
with love and kind words,
streaming from
your hose of a mouth.

Damp by droplets of adoration,
even so,
weeds fill my thoughts,
creeping in steadily,
and I wonder,
when we bloom,
do we bloom into blossoms
or bruises?

Sarah Blakely

Possessed By Happiness

Who is this girl inside of me?
Who stepped in the moment I could
        breathe?
Who is she with a smile so bright?
Who is she to forget the ways I fight?

She is the golden apple, happiness,
she is never around for my nastiness,
she glosses over my festering wounds,
she has no fear as she howls at the moon.

Sturdy As My Favorite Necklace

Cheap, foreign, plain,
yet strong and beautiful.
Unique design and curves,
blue and black,
like the bruises on my body
lined in silver and strung on my neck.
Who knew such weak materials
could be so strong in the end?
After being tugged, thrown around.
Two silver crescents hang from darkness
like the moon through my window.
Sharp at the edges, like fangs,
biting at my tongue, threatening,
keep quiet.
Through tears and rain,
through blood and rust,
through silver bars.
But am I safe now?
Sturdy as ever,
simply a little worn.

About The Author

Sarah Blakely is a poet and songwriter based on the central coast of California.
She writes primarily about her own experiences with trauma and relationships as well as struggles with mental health and healing from trauma.
Her debut collection, *Volcano Girl*, was released in April 2022, and deals specifically with sexual trauma, developing PTSD, and the healing journey that follows.

Scan the code below with your phone to be directed to my website, SoundCloud, and more!